How to Shock Your Parents

Mick Gowar

OXFORD
UNIVERSITY PRESS

OXFORD
UNIVERSITY PRESS

Great Clarendon Street, Oxford OX2 6DP

Oxford University Press is a department of the University of Oxford.
It furthers the University's objective of excellence in research, scholarship,
and education by publishing worldwide in

Oxford   New York

Auckland Cape Town Dar es Salaam Hong Kong Karachi
Kuala Lumpur Madrid Melbourne Mexico City Nairobi
New Delhi Shanghai Taipei Toronto

With offices in

Argentina Austria Brazil Chile Czech Republic France Greece
Guatemala Hungary Italy Japan Poland Portugal Singapore
South Korea Switzerland Thailand Turkey Ukraine Vietnam

Oxford is a registered trade mark of Oxford University Press
in the UK and in certain other countries

Text © Mick Gowar 2005

The moral rights of the author have been asserted

Database right Oxford University Press (maker)

First published 2005

All rights reserved. No part of this publication may be reproduced,
stored in a retrieval system, or transmitted, in any form or by any means,
without the prior permission in writing of Oxford University Press,
or as expressly permitted by law, or under terms agreed with the appropriate
reprographics rights organization. Enquiries concerning reproduction
outside the scope of the above should be sent to the Rights Department,
Oxford University Press, at the address above

You must not circulate this book in any other binding or cover
and you must impose this same condition on any acquirer

British Library Cataloguing in Publication Data

Data available

ISBN 978-0-19-919880-1

11 13 15 17 19 20 18 16 14 12

Printed in China by Imago

Acknowledgements

The publisher would like to thank the following for permission to reproduce photographs:
Title page OUP; **p7** Mary Evans Picture Library; **p10** John Frost Newspapers Limited; **p11** Corbis/Henry Diltz;
p12 John Frost Newspapers Limited; **p13** Associated Press; **p14** Moviestore Collection; **p15**t Sony Music/
Pennie Smith.com, b Allstar Photo Agency; **p17** Redferns Music Picture Library; **p18** Rex Features; **p19**t
Redferns Music Picture Library/Michael Ochs Archives, b Moviestore Collection; **p20** Rex Features;
p21 Redferns Music Picture Library; **p22**t Rex Features, c and b Redferns Music Picture Library;
p23 Rex Features/Sipa Press; **p24**t Getty Editorial, b Corbis/Toby Melville; **p25**t Starfile/Mick Rock,
b Rex Features; **p26** Rex Features; **p27** Redferns Music Pictures Library

Cover photograph: Alamy/Don Jon Red

Illustrations by Martin Aston

Extract from 'Blue Suede Shoes' by Carl Perkins, copyright © Carl Perkins (Carl Perkins Music Inc.),
reprinted by permission of MPL Communications Ltd.

'Laver's Law' compiled by James Laver, reprinted by permission of David Higham Associates Ltd.

Every effort has been made to contact copyright holders of material reproduced in this book.
If notified, the publishers will be pleased to rectify any errors or omissions
at the earliest opportunity.

CONTENTS

ᴇᴀRLY shocks!

In **medieval** times, the shortness of men's skirts and tunics and the length of the toes on their shoes were thought so outrageous that laws were passed to stop these fashions.

Throughout history, priests have preached **sermons** telling young people that they would go to hell for all eternity if they wore certain clothes, or listened to certain music, or danced a certain way.

TRY THIS QUIZ ON A FRIEND –
OR MAYBE ON YOUR TEACHER

Which of these was a fashion law at sometime?

- It was illegal for any man to wear shoes with toes more than two inches long.
- Only a princess or duchess was allowed to wear clothes made of silk.
- Only a man who owned goods worth £200 or more was allowed to wear a silk scarf.
- It was illegal to wear clothes fastened with buttons.

That was a trick question – all of those have been laws at some time during the Middle Ages, in Europe.

Henry Tudor – Superstar

There were music and fashion stars in the past. Five hundred years ago the boy pin-up of Europe was Prince Henry of England. He was tall, slim and gorgeously good looking. He could fight, sing and write poetry. He even wrote hit songs like *Pastime with Good Company* – it was even rumoured that he'd written the international hit *Greensleeves*. It was a shame that gorgeous Prince Henry grew up to be the fat and murderous Henry VIII who had people's heads chopped off!

There's a big difference between the youth fashions of the middle ages and the youth fashions of now. Medieval fashions were only for the rich – courtiers, knights, lords and ladies. Ordinary working people wore home-made clothes, just like their fathers and mothers had worn, *and* like their grandparents, great-grandparents and their great-great grandparents.

In the 20th century, for the first time in history, ordinary, working people could afford to buy fashionable clothes. The invention of the phonograph (or record player), radio and television, and the CD player meant that more and more people listened to and enjoyed the latest music.

7

Watch out, watch out — there's a Teddy about!

Rock'n'Roll started in the 1950s. It was music anyone could listen to and anyone could play. You didn't need to study music for years and years to enjoy or play Rock'n'Roll.

Like the Blues music of America, early Rock'n'Roll was based on only three guitar chords.

Learn these chords and *you* can play Rock'n'Roll!

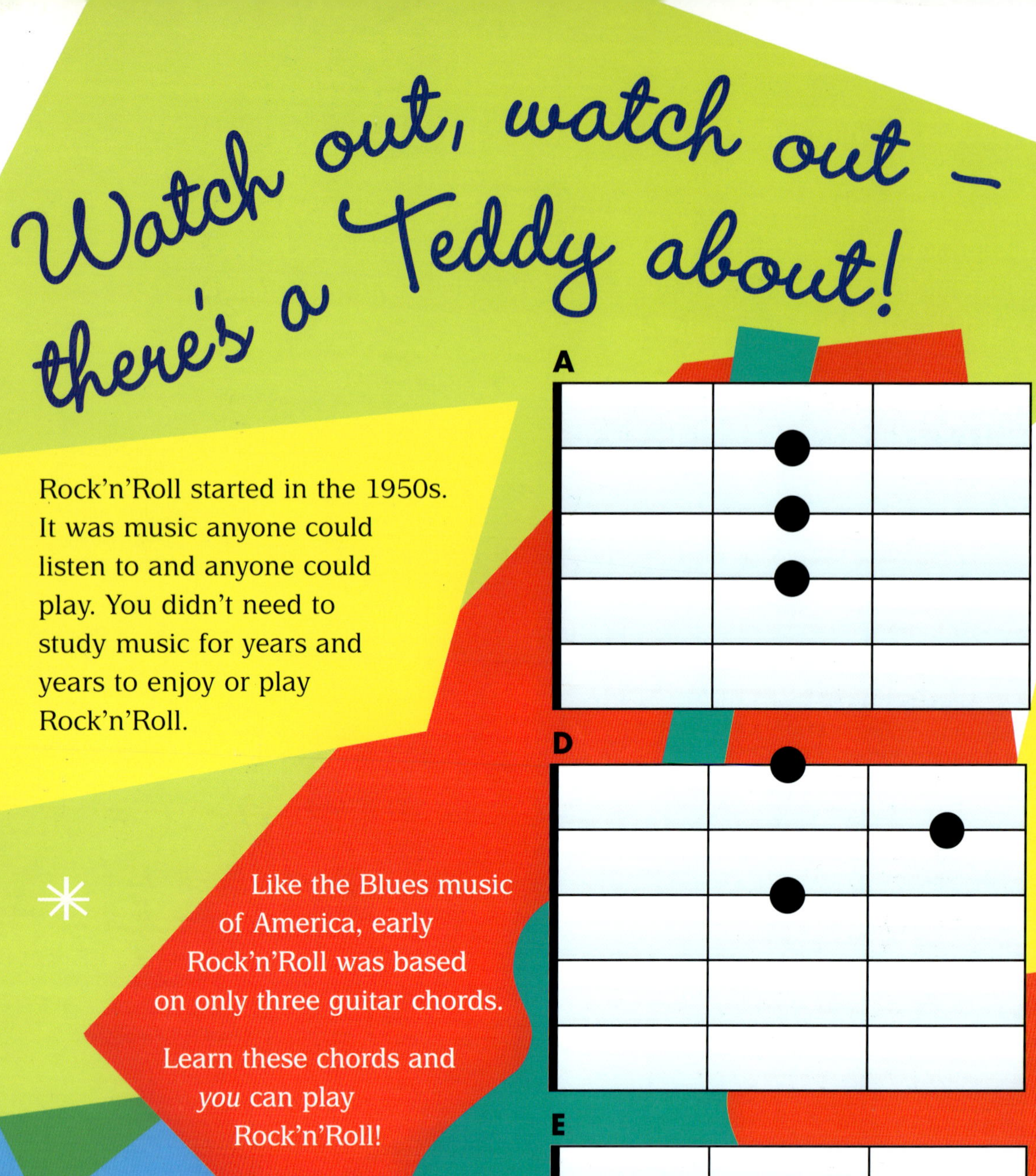

Early Rock'n'Roll music was loud and angry. Many young men who were Rock'n'Roll fans rode motorbikes, wore leather jackets and combed their hair into big greasy quiffs.

Others wore thick-soled suede shoes and trousers that were so tight they were called 'drainpipes'. They also wore long, velvet-collared jackets, of the style worn in Edwardian times, and so they were called 'Teddy Boys'.

One of the first Rock'n'Roll songs was about someone's blue suede shoes.

You can knock me down, step on my face
Slander my name all over the place.
Do anything that you wanna do
But uh uh honey lay off of my shoes...
You can do anything but don't step on my
blue suede shoes.

Lots of parents, teachers, vicars and politicians were horrified by the Teddy Boys and Rock'n'Rollers. The newspapers of the late 1950s were full of stories of Teddy Boys fighting and ripping up the seats at theatres where there were Rock'n'Roll shows.

So all the parents and politicians who hated the Teddy Boys would be really happy if young people wanted peace and love and no more fighting... wouldn't they?

All you need is love!

No! Parents and politicians who hated the Teddy Boys weren't at all happy when young people wanted peace and love and no more fighting… When the hippy fashion came in the late 1960s parents hated it!

Hippies grew their hair long, and men and women wore beads. Some wore long Indian-style robes with flowery patterns, called *kaftans*. Hippies wanted everyone to be gentle and kind to each other. A famous hippy slogan was: *Make Love Not War.*

What worried politicians was that hippies didn't want to work in big companies, and they especially didn't want to go into the army.

This caused a lot of trouble in America, where the hippie movement began. All American boys in the 1960s had to serve in the army, and many were sent to fight in Vietnam where America was involved in a war. Many hippies refused to join the army and fight.

Instead of being fast and angry, rock songs became slow and dreamy. Instead of being about motorbikes and blue suede shoes, the new songs were about love and peace and flowers. A lot of hippy music was influenced by the music of India and the East.

George Harrison, of The Beatles, playing a sitar during a trip to study Indian religion.

Quiz Time!

Was Your Gran a Hippy? (or Your Grandad?)

Ask someone you know who was a teenager in the 1960s these questions:

1. Did you own a kaftan or a tie-dyed 'grandad' vest?
2. Did you ever wear a necklace with a little bell on it?
3. Did you ever wear an Afghan goatskin coat?
4. Did you ever go out wearing flowers in your hair – and you weren't being a bridesmaid?
5. Did you ever wear spectacles or sunglasses with little round gold frames?
6. Did you ever go to a free pop festival?
7. Did you use to dance with your hands waving above your head as if you were swatting flies?

If they answered 'Yes' to five or more questions they *were* a hippy (even if they won't admit it).

The biggest craze in pop music in the late 1970s was the complete opposite of the gentle dreamy songs of the hippies: it was called 'Punk' rock.

Like early Rock'n'Rollers, many of the Punk bands were teenagers writing songs about what they thought really mattered to other teenagers. Instead of writing about love and peace and magic **gnomes**, Punk songs were about how difficult it was to get a job, or how boring life was for young people – especially if they weren't living near London or one of the big cities.

Punk was loud and simple – just drums, bass and guitar, playing the old three-chord songs, like early Rock'n'Roll. It was also very aggressive. So were the Punks: at Punk concerts it was considered quite normal for the audience to spit at the members of the band they were watching!

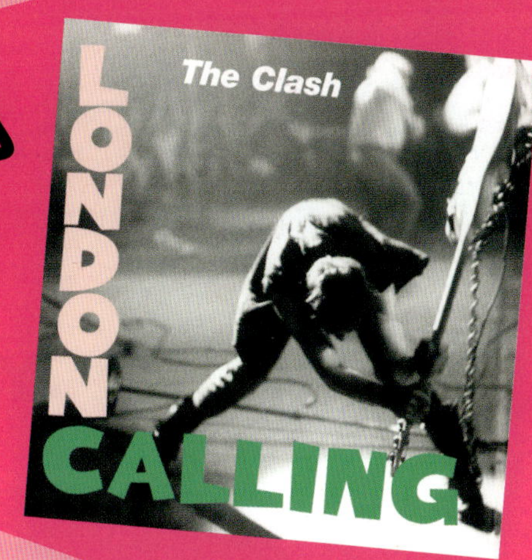

DID YOU KNOW?

Most pop performers nowadays are expected to be extremely good looking, and very athletic. But one of the greatest Punk songwriters and singers was disabled.

His name was Ian Dury. He caught **Polio** when he was seven years old, and spent most of his childhood either in hospital or in a special school for disabled children.

He studied at Art School. He formed a band called 'The Blockheads' in 1977.

Ian wrote lots of comedy songs about people living in Essex and East London, but his biggest hits were songs to dance to like *Hit Me with Your Rhythm Stick*.

Ian used his fame to raise money for disabled children, and to campaign for Polio vaccination in poorer countries.

PUNK FASHION

Punk wasn't just a musical style, it was also a fashion style. Like Punk music, Punk clothes were supposed to shock older people.

The Punk Look

hair shaved at the sides, top combed up to form a 'Mohican' crest which is kept upright with lots of hair gel

ears and nose pierced – unusual in the 1970s, safety pins worn instead of rings or studs

necklace made from chain and padlock

T-shirt – deliberately ripped and 'mended' with safety pins

short tartan skirt, deliberately frayed around the hem torn, black fishnet tights

Dr Marten workman's boots

What could possibly follow Punk?

New Romantic

What followed Punk in the late 1970s was a style of music and clothes that was the complete opposite of the rough, aggressive Punk style. It was called 'New Romantic'.

New Romantics looked as if they'd dressed from a dressing-up box, or the costume cupboard of a theatre. New Romantics wanted to look like old-fashioned pirates and highwaymen!

The New Romantic Look

hair grown long, coloured, elaborately waved and sprayed to stay in place

elaborate make-up – for boys as well as girls

wide-sleeved 'duelling' style shirt with lace collar and cuffs

long, 18th century-style waistcoat

breeches

pirate boots

New Romantic fashion started in the most expensive clubs and discos in London. It began with a small group of people competing with each other to look more and more outrageous. Unlike Punk, it started as a fashion for rich people who could afford to go to the trendiest clubs. New Romantic music was dance music, with a regular, pulsing beat – just right for discos and night clubs. But just like Punk, New Romantic fashion was supposed to shock, but in a completely different way.

Did You Know?

The same designer created both the Punk and New Romantic looks? Her name is Vivienne Westwood. She designed the Punk look – the torn t-shirt 'mended' with safety pins, and black combat trousers decorated with extra zips and straps. She also invented the New Romantic 'pirate' look.

Vivienne Westwood has also designed clothes in cowboy style and clothes supposed to make people look like the Queen – tweed skirts worn with hats in the shape of crowns.

Vivienne Westwood

Adam from 'Adam and the Ants', a New Romantic pop group.

DISCO

Disco clubs, playing Top 20 records (instead of music by a live band), had been popular in British towns and cities since the late 1960s. But Disco music and fashion really took off in 1977 when the film *Saturday Night Fever* was released. It was the story of a group of young friends in New York with dead-end jobs and boring lives. The only thing they looked forward to was going to the local disco on Saturday night.

Did You Know?

Madonna went to University to study classical dance before becoming a singer?

In fact, Madonna was such a great ballet dancer that she was given a special **scholarship** to Michigan University in the USA. Then she went to New York, where she discovered Disco. But her first big break into show business wasn't in America. It was in France, in a show called *Disco Revue* in Paris.

When she went back to New York from Paris, she tried singing with several bands before releasing her fist solo single *Holiday* in 1983.

Madonna Multiple Choice

1 How many Top 40 hits has Madonna had in the UK?

- 25
- 37
- 58

2 Which film does Madonna not appear in?

- Evita
- Desperately Seeking Susan
- Die Another Day
- Funny Girl

3 How many albums and CDs has Madonna sold?

- 25 million
- 60 million
- 130 million

4 What's the name of Madonna's son?

- Rocco
- Chico
- Harpo
- Groucho

Answers on page 32

Band Aid and Live Aid

In 1984 a dreadful **famine** began in the East African country of Ethiopia. At first, many Western governments – including Britain's – didn't want to help Ethiopia. They said the famine was the fault of the Ethiopian government.

In October 1984 a BBC reporter, Michael Buerk, went to Ethiopia and filmed children and adults starving to death. When his report was shown on BBC Television, many people who saw it were so shocked they wanted to do something to help the people of Ethiopia. One of those people was the Irish rock singer Bob Geldof.

He thought that the best way to raise money was to record a special song and send all the money from the record to Ethiopia. So Bob and another rock musician, Midge Ure, wrote *Do They Know It's Christmas?*

The two musicians booked a recording studio, then they phoned all the famous musicians and singers they knew and invited them to sing and play on the record.

Forty of the best-known British and Irish pop stars made the record in a single day. They called themselves 'Band Aid'.

After the success of the Band Aid record, Bob Geldof decided to try to raise even more money for Ethiopia. So he organized *Live Aid*: two concerts, on the same day – one in Britain, at Wembley Stadium and one in the USA, with many of the most famous pop stars of the time performing. It was shown on TV all over the world to over 1.5 billion people and lasted for sixteen hours. At the last estimate, it had raised over $100 million!

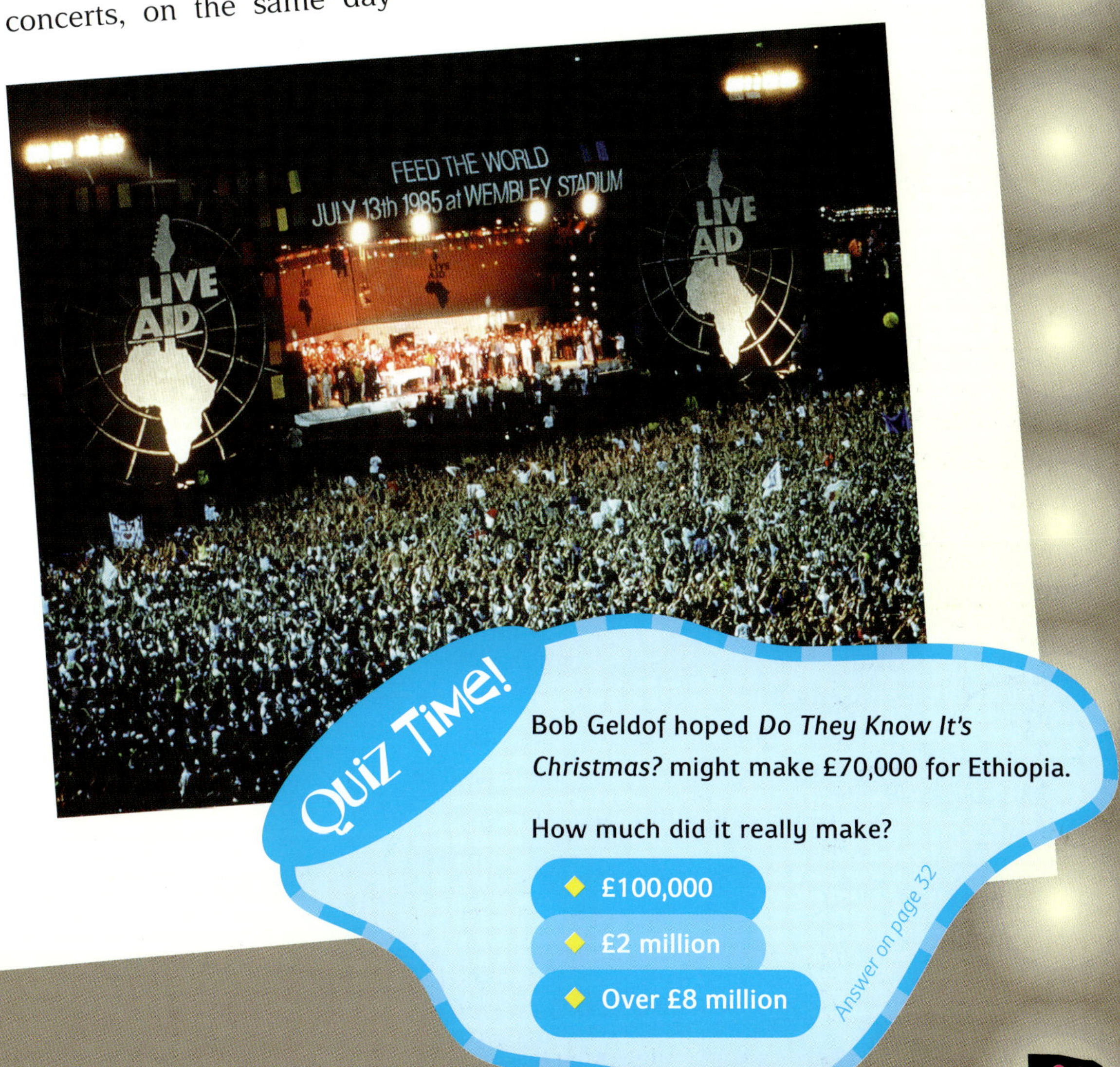

Quiz Time!

Bob Geldof hoped *Do They Know It's Christmas?* might make £70,000 for Ethiopia.

How much did it really make?

- ◆ £100,000
- ◆ £2 million
- ◆ Over £8 million

Answer on page 32

Band Aid 20

In 2004 a new version of *Do They Know It's Christmas?* was recorded. Again it featured the most famous pop stars of the time, with some of the pop stars from the original recording. This time the musicians were called *Band Aid 20* as it was twenty years since the first *Band Aid*.

The song had not lost any of its appeal. Just as in 1984, it was at number one in the charts for many weeks. Twenty years after Bob Geldof and Midge Ure had written the song, it was still making lots of money to help people in Africa.

Queen

The English band Queen were one of the big hits of *Live Aid*. Their most famous songs were mostly big, sing-along numbers like *We Are The Champions* and *We Will Rock You*, which were perfect for performing at Wembley Stadium, where the UK concert was held.

Queen had been formed in 1970. In 1975 they made what a lot of people think was the first pop video, for their single *Bohemian Rhapsody*. The band stopped playing live when their lead singer, Freddie Mercury, died in 1991. But their music is still very popular, thanks to the musical play *We Will Rock You* which is based on Queen's songs.

Hip Hop

It's hard now to imagine a time when there weren't rappers and star DJs. But Hip Hop only began in the late 1970s at the time when Punk started. It all began with one teenage boy from Jamaica…

Clive Campbell arrived in New York from Jamaica when he was only 18 years old. At the time, Disco music was the big craze in New York, but the fashionable Disco clubs were too expensive for Clive and his friends to get into. So Clive started his own 'parties', calling himself 'DJ Kool Herc'. He played records through the sort of huge sound system popular in Jamaica. He also used two record decks so the music never stopped. Amazingly, no one in New York seems to have thought of this before. Clive became the 'father' of Hip Hop music.

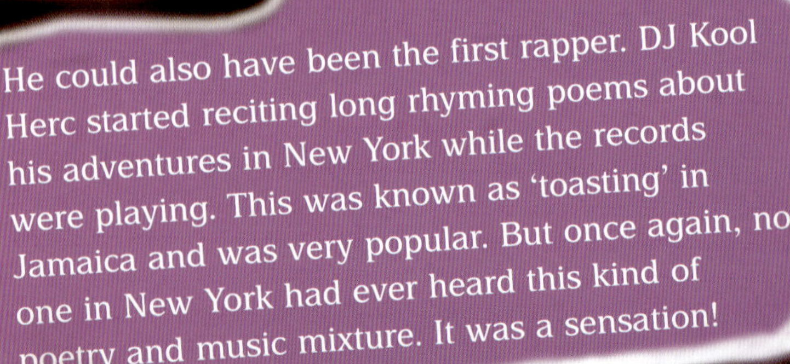

He could also have been the first rapper. DJ Kool Herc started reciting long rhyming poems about his adventures in New York while the records were playing. This was known as 'toasting' in Jamaica and was very popular. But once again, no one in New York had ever heard this kind of poetry and music mixture. It was a sensation!

Grandmaster Flash and the Furious Five

Formed in New York in 1976, 'Grandmaster Flash and the Furious Five' was one of the first rap bands. Grandmaster Flash was the DJ behind the band. He invented many modern DJ techniques. He invented 'needle dropping' which involved using two copies of the same record to play the drum 'breaks' or solos over and over again, creating a new live version or 'mix'. He also invented the technique of 'scratching' – sliding a record rapidly backwards and forwards under the needle to produce an electric shaker sound.

Shocking... or what?

Every new fashion and type of music has shocked people – at the time. Women's skirts that showed the ankle, dancing the waltz – in the past people have thought these were outrageous. Nowadays, they seem old-fashioned and boring, while modern fashions look exciting and shocking. But some time in the future, today's fashions will look as old-fashioned as men wearing top hats and women wearing dresses with bustles at the back.

James Laver, a favourite costume historian, who was also responsible for the costume department at the *Victoria and Albert Museum* in London – the world's greatest collection of fashion from all periods of history – came up with the following table. It shows how long it takes for fashion to stop being shocking.

This table's a warning to you, too. One day your children – or even your grandchildren – will find an old photo of you wearing what you think today are really cool clothes and they'll laugh and laugh! But don't worry – that's fashion!

Laver's Law

What people say	What it means
Indecent	It's ten years before its time
Shameless	It's five years before its time
Daring	It's one year before its time
Smart	Today's fashion
Dowdy	It's one year after its time
Hideous	It's ten years after its time
Ridiculous	It's 20 years after its time
Amusing	It's 50 years after its time
Quaint	It's 70 years after its time
Romantic	It's 100 years after its time
Beautiful	It's 150 years after its time

Recommended Listening

Early shocks!

Pastime With Good Company, performed by Poeme Harmonique, on the CD *Pastime With Good Company,* on the *Alpha* label

For a great collection of medieval songs and dances try *Miri It Is* by The Dufay Collective, on New Direction

Watch out, watch out – there's a Teddy about!

Listen to the original *Blue Suede Shoes* recorded by the composer, Carl Perkins, on his album *Blue Suede Shoes, PIE*

And Elvis Presley at his best: *Heartbreak Hotel,* from *Elvis 30 No 1 Hits, RCA*

Also highly recommended for Rock'n'Rollers:

C'mon Everybody by Eddie Cochrane from *The Best of Eddie Cochrane,* EMI

Rave On by Buddy Holly from *The Very Best of Buddy Holly,* Universal

All you need is love!

Here's a short selection of some of the best songs from the late 1960s:

Light My Fire by The Doors from *The Best of The Doors,* Warner

Truckin' by The Grateful Dead from *The Very Best of The Grateful Dead,* WSM

Good Vibrations by The Beach Boys from *The Very Best of The Beach Boys,* Capitol.

The Beatles, of course: *Lucy In The Sky With Diamonds* and *A Day In The Life* from *Sgt Pepper's Lonely Hearts Club Band,* The Beatles, Parlophone

And the best **progressive rock**: *Close To The Edge* from the album of the same name by Yes, on Atlantic

Punk

London Calling, The Clash, from *London Calling,* Columbia

Two of Ian Dury's greatest songs: *Hit Me With Your Rhythm Stick* and *Reasons To Be Cheerful Part 3* from *Do It Yourself,* released by Edsel

Some great music that came immediately after Punk:

A Town Called Malice and *That's Entertainment* by The Jam from *The Very Best Of The Jam*, Polydor

Pump It Up by Elvis Costello from *The Very Best Of Elvis Costello*, UMTV

New Romantic

Prince Charming by Adam And The Ants from *The Very Best Of Adam and The Ants*, Columbia

Vienna by Ultravox from *Vienna*, EMI

Girls On Film by Duran Duran from *Greatest*, EMI

Disco

Recommended disco classics:

Holiday and *Into The Groove* by Madonna from The Immaculate Collection, Warner

Staying Alive by The BeeGees, from the soundtrack album to *Saturday Night Fever*, Polydor

I Will Survive by Gloria Gaynor, from *The Disco Album*, Sony

Band Aid and Live Aid

The best way to understand what this was about is to watch the three DVD set *Live Aid*, which includes the video for the original recording of *Do They Know It's Christmas?*

Hip Hop!

Grandmaster Flash and the Furious Five/The Sugar Hill Gang *The Greatest Hits*, Sanctuary

Glossary

famine – a severe shortage of food which results in large numbers of people starving

gnomes – mythical, woodland creatures, related to pixies and elves, who are thought to look like tiny old men with long-white beards

medieval – a word used to describe anything to do with the middle ages (approx AD 800 to 1500)

Polio – short for poliomyelitis, a virus which can attack the nervous system causing paralysis and breathing difficulties

Progressive Rock – a form of rock music which mixed rock 'n' roll, folk and classical music together and was popular in the late 1960s and early 1970s

scholarship – a special gift, usually of money, to help someone particularly talented to study a subject at university

sermon – a talk on a religious or moral subject which is given by a priest or religious leader as part of a religious service

Index

Quiz Time! Answers

Page 21
1. 58 2. *Funny Girl* 3. 130 million 4. Rocco

Page 23
Over £8 million